How t Your Soulmate on the Internet

NOT!

The Hilarious Guide for Women on How to Avoid the Dangers of Internet Dating Scammers

Jennifer Fallon

snapping turtle
snappingturtlebooks.com

Published in 2013
by Snapping Turtle Books

Copyright © 2013 Jennifer Fallon

Snapping Turtle Ltd.
PO Box 638, Rangiora, Canterbury, 7440
New Zealand

Cover design by David Tonkin
Cover Images: shutterstock.com

All rights reserved

ISBN: 1494226057
ISBN-13: 978-1494226053

CONTENTS

	Foreword	v
1	Scammer V The Impatient Writer	Pg 7
2	Scammer V The Widow - With Tropical Fruit	Pg 9
3	Scammer V The Mathematician	Pg 19
4	Scammer V Jessica Rabbit	Pg 20
5	Scammer V The High Priestess	Pg 23
6	Scammer V The Astronaut. With Goats.	Pg 29
7	Scammer V Hilary Clinton... In Klingon	Pg 34
8	Scammer V Transgender 87 Year-Old	Pg 47
9	Very Focused Scammer V The Dominatrix... And The Cia	Pg 57
10	Scammer V The Interpol Investigator	Pg 67
11	Scammer V The Jail Bird	Pg 71
12	Scammer V The Interpol Investigator	Pg 67
13	Scammer V The Grammar Nazi	Pg 71
14	Scammer v I Don't Have Time For This Anymore	Pg 82
15	How do I spot a Scammer on Facebook?	Pg 83

FOREWORD

I have the dubious honor of being female, widowed, and have a Facebook page. I have a couple of them actually. I am a writer, a public figure, and there's no avoiding it.

I also friend everyone who asks, because I am a writer and I assume (or at least I used to assume) people were friending me because they were fans.

Turns out I sit squarely in the middle of the prime demographic for catfish scammers.

I find it more than a little bit sad that there are so many women out there, around my age, who are so desperate for some sort of validation, or who are so determined to find a partner, that an entire industry has grown up around their vulnerability.

I get three to four of these "looking for love" type messages a day. I used to delete them. But then I started answering them, as I realized that while they think they're stringing *me* along, they are leaving someone more vulnerable alone.

And it's fun.

This book is the result of popular demand. I used to post these conversations on my Facebook page. (Even funnier when you think the men targeting me could work out

I'm playing them if they so much as read a single entry on my page.) We have complied them here at the request of my readers, for your entertainment.

I hope you enjoy... there's plenty more out there.

And if you know someone you think might get taken in by one of these catfishers, give them this book. They might get a laugh. Hopefully, they'll learn how disturbingly common catfishers' methods are.

Jennifer Fallon

Disclaimer
The names featured in this book are the names used by the scammers on their social media profiles. These are fake names which have been stolen by the scammers to make them appear "real". The inclusion of these names is not intended to cause insult or suggest in any way that someone who shares one of these names is a scammer themselves.

1. Scammer v The Impatient Writer

Henry Paul

I have been so doubtful that you will accept a request from someone you are not familiar with, especially someone who has so much interest in you. so I was really happy when you did accept me. I am an arbitrator and a mediator based in manchester. I have been attracted to you and so interested in meeting you. because of some certain feelings I have for you. Please, if you do not mind i will like us to have a chat. to know our selves better. I will really like to hear from you.

Jennifer Fallon

Only interested if you are rich. I need money.

Henry Paul

so tell me

how was your night?

Jennifer Fallon

Spent it friending about 30 other dipshits just like you who have fallen in love with me too, based on a photo that isn't really me. I am very popular. Don't contact me again unless you can send me large amounts of cash.

Henry Paul

so tell how much do you need you need

Jennifer Fallon

A million dollars would be good.

Henry Paul

what do yoiu need such a whole money for ?

Jennifer Fallon

To fund my hobby of scamming assholes who try to steal money from vulnerable women by pretending they love them on Facebook

Henry Paul

ops that is bad

but you should not be hard on me cause i am not one ok

Jennifer Fallon

Bored now... go away

Henry Paul

i do not understand you

2. Scammer V The Widow - With Tropical Fruit

Roland Williams

> Hello? I am William from UK, but i live in India presently, I went through your profile and it was beautiful as you. Please I will love to know you better.William.

Roland Williams

> Thank of respond

Jennifer Fallon

> Wow... what was it in particular that attracted you?

Roland Williams

> Thanks Jennifer for your reply.. Your profile attract me.. the beautiful face, and the smile..

Jennifer Fallon

> Yes, but you said you went through my profile and you thought it was as beautiful as me.

What did I write about myself that you find so beguiling?

I don't want a partner who is only interested in me because of my outstanding beauty.

Roland Williams

i am here to know you more better
as we are friends
it will be good to know more about
ourselves
so am here to know you

Jennifer Fallon

But you said you liked my profile. You must know lots about me if you read it. What did you like about it?

Roland Williams

i know you are widowed
born in august 4th
lived in New Zealand
seem some of your beautiful photos
aswell

Jennifer Fallon

> So what did you find so beautiful, other than my photo? My birthday? That I live NZ? Or that my husband is dead. You said my profile is as beautiful as me. Does that mean you think I look like a date, a country or a corpse?

Roland Williams

> yes
> you look likea date
> but first we have to know more about ourselves

Jennifer Fallon

> Really... you think I look like a date? A brown and wrinkly and dried out? That's insulting.

Roland Williams

> no
> that's not what i mean
> i simply means we might have something good in common
> let me tell you some things about me

Jennifer Fallon

> You said I look like a tropical fruit. What sort of future can I have with a man like that?
> I'd much rather be an avocado. Or a banana.

Roland Williams

> i never insultd you dear

Jennifer Fallon

> You are a nut, I think
> You called me a date.

Roland Williams

> Hahaha

Jennifer Fallon

> I am not laughing

Roland Williams

> dear i said we might have a date

Jennifer Fallon

Why would I date you?

Roland Williams

i said might
please gt me well

Jennifer Fallon

Oh, so now I'm not good enough for you>
YOu only MIGHT want to date me? I can;t
take much more of this abuse. First you
tell me my profile that says my husband is
dead makes you think I'm beautiful, which
is really quite sick and twisted, when you
think about it, and now you're not sure if
you want to date me. My mother was
right, being filthy rich just doesn't buy you
happiness.

Roland Williams

few things about mei like most of all sorts
of outdoor activities; gardening, fishing,
cycling, walking, cooking and general
overall puttering. Very fun loving and
spontaneous. I enjoy stimulating
conversations with intellectual individuals.
But I also like being silly and non-

intellectual at times. I love amusement parks and white water rafting. My dream vacation is to go to St. Johns, USVI. I enjoy the occasional mixed drink or glass of wine. I don't care for senseless piercings and tattoos but one or two are ok. Love long drives to no where and long romantic weekends at the beach, I believe this will tell much, ask more if you want to know, I will be gladly to tell...Hugs

Roland Williams

might becuase we dont know ourself

Jennifer Fallon

You like white water rafting? My husband died in a white water rafting accident. I could never get involved with someone who did that again. Much too painful.

Roland Williams

hey i never say so
i said you are widow
please friend do try to read with understanding..
sorry

Jennifer Fallon

You did say so. I asked you what you thought was beautiful about me and you said you knew I was a widow. That means you think it's beautiful that my husband died. That is sick.

Roland Williams

no
no
no
dont thnk so
that was never my meaning
you asked what did i see on your profile
i told you few things that i found there
i am not a wicked man

Jennifer Fallon

Then you are not very bright because that is what you wrote

Roland Williams

to wish anybody death
sorry
and sorry if it hurts you

never my intention hurting anyone
am sorry

Jennifer Fallon

Sorry is not good enough. Please go away.

Roland Williams

d the conversation agian from the beginning

Jennifer Fallon

Alright then... what is your name?

Roland Williams

Am Roland

Jennifer Fallon

Are you sure?

Roland Williams

Full name Roland Williams
waht?

Jennifer Fallon

> You look an awful lot like this guy: https://www.facebook.com/jorgen.dehlin?hc_location=timeline [Link to identical profile, different name]

Roland Williams

> let me see

Jennifer Fallon

> So which one of you is the scammer... you or Jorgen? Or is he you as well?

Roland Williams

> what
> i dont get you

Jennifer Fallon

> My... what an interesting IP address you have too...

Roland Williams

> Punck ass why you call me scammer
> you fake too
> You know what
> go fuck yourself

guess you hqve sex toil at home
hahaha you use it huh
PUNK ASS

3. Scammer V The Mathematician

Mark Smith

Hello miss how are u doing today

Mark Smith

Hi miss

Jennifer Fallon

Who are you?

Mark Smith

Who are u too

Jennifer Fallon

What do you want. I'm busy

Mark Smith

I dont need anything from u ok MISS RIGHT

Jennifer Fallon

Then why are you contacting me?

Mark Smith

I cant remember adding up who did

4. Scammer V Jessica Rabbit

Davision Smith

> Hello dear
>
> Thanks for Accepting me as a friend

Jennifer Fallon

> Are you a fan of my work?

Davision Smith

> How are u doing today

Jennifer Fallon

> Hi. Are you a fan?

Davision Smith

> Yes miss and i think i love work so much

Jennifer Fallon

> Which of my books did you like the best? And why? Do you find it is the esoteric nature of the worlds I create or the complex, Machiavellian machinations of the antagonists?

Davision Smith

> Swell i have read so many of ur books lately and to tell u the true i find them so interesting

Jennifer Fallon

> How many did you read? Who was your favourite character?

Davision Smith

> Swell when i read this book made by u Lord of shadows,Lion of senet I enjoy reading those books so much

Jennifer Fallon

> What did you like about them? My favourite character was Jessica Rabbit.

Davision Smith

> Well i love the Action the love and too my favorite was Jessica Rabbit too

Jennifer Fallon

> You moron... there in no Jessica Rabbit in that book!
>
> You haven't read a single word I've written. How silly of me to think any fan of mine would write with such poor grammar and so many occurrences of the word "swell".
>
> I do not wish to speak to you again.
>
> When you have read all 17 of my books and all the

anthologies in which I have other works, I might consider speaking to you again. By the time you have read all of the above, not only will you will know more words in English, but also that Jessica Rabbit is a cartoon character.

I do hope you are not planning a career of scamming women on Facebook. You will starve. You are really not very good at it all, are you?

5. Scammer V The High Priestess

Robert Cole

Hello Pretty , how are you doing today am Robert by name am single and searching just joined Facebook am just going through profiles finding friends when i came across yours and will love to know you more better if you don't mind..?

Jennifer Fallon

Hello

Robert Cole

How are you doing today , and thanks so much for accepting my friend request.

Jennifer Fallon

I accept everyone's requests. I have no standards.

Robert Cole

I am robert by name am new on facebook am also a widower.

For some years now

Jennifer Fallon

Are you a DICK (Daring, Intelligent, Charming and Kind) or a KNOB (Kind, Nice, Ordinary Bloke)?

Robert Cole

>Lol am a DICK

>Jennifer Fallon

>Oh, you most assuredly are!

Robert Cole

>Thanks

>You are beautiful

Jennifer Fallon

>I could tell you were a dick, just from the way you introduced yourself.

Robert Cole

>Really so tell me are you single ?

Jennifer Fallon

>Only on Tuesdays. I have boyfriends for every other day of the week. They are mostly dicks, but there are a few knobs in there too.

Robert Cole

>Your profile says you are widowed

Jennifer Fallon

I am. Makes it a lot easier to juggle all those boyfriends since my husband died.

Robert Cole

I see

are you a christian?

Jennifer Fallon

I belong to the Church of St Sarcasm. We worship Earth Worms. Worm Blessings to you, brother.

Robert Cole

Do you believe in God?

Jennifer Fallon

Do you believe in God?

Robert Cole

Yes do you?

Jennifer Fallon

I believe in Earth Worms. They are the true gods of the universe. They replenish the earth, they do no harm. And they taste good with ketchup.

Worm Blessings to you brother

Robert Cole

So have you ever thought of getting into a serious relationship?

Jennifer Fallon

Sure, but only with a member of my church. Would you be willing to become a Worm for me?

Robert Cole

A worm?

Jennifer Fallon

That's what we call members of our church. New members are worms. If you pass all the initiation tests you can work your way up to a Slug.

I wasn't going to mention it just yet, because we've only just met, but I am actually the High Priestess. You would have to do the tests, and pay the fees, but if you can handle the pain, and can afford it, we might be onto something here.

Worm blessings to you brother

Robert Cole

How could you be into that such of a thing , am widow and don't want those kind of things in life , what are the gain in it..?

Jennifer Fallon

> So you are a bigot, then? You have no tolerance for other people's religious beliefs.

Robert Cole

> I have but this is different

Jennifer Fallon

> I am really offended that you have dissed my beliefs.
>
> I don't want to talk to you any longer. Besides, another man named Justin Case just messaged me and told me I'm pretty, too. Maybe he'll be more respectful of other people's beliefs than you are.

Robert Cole

> This is cruel
>
> How can you just come to that conclusion.?
>
> I guess you are just searching for men to bring too your religion

Jennifer Fallon

> Your exact words - "How could you be into that such of a thing , am widow and don't want those kind of things in life".

You are implying that there is something wrong with what I do. Fine. If you don't want those kinds of things in your life, go away. Justin is better looking than you, anyway, and he owns a Porche. He can afford to start Stage One of Worm, too.

He is a knob.

Robert Cole

May God forgive you

I guess , you take from people and you can't help people , its not good

Jennifer Fallon

Would you like to send a donation?

Worm Blessings to you brother

6. Scammer V The Astronaut. With Goats.

Roland Gibert

> Hi

Jennifer Fallon

> Hi

Roland Gibert

> How you doing today ?

Jennifer Fallon

> I'm OK. Do you like Goats?

Roland Gibert

> Hehehehe why you ask yea I do

Jennifer Fallon

> I'm doing a scientific thesis on goats survivability in space for NASA. They are thinking of putting them into the International Space Station as a renewable food source. Just wondering if you knew anything about them?
>
> You look like someone who might have feelings for goats.

Roland Gibert

Wow nice yea I do so where you from ?

Jennifer Fallon

Do you really have feelings for goats! That's so cool. How long have you had this thing for goats?

Roland Gibert

Been a long time because am always busy with my job now

Jennifer Fallon

Do you work with goats or just socialize with them?

Roland Gibert

Just socialize with them am a salior I work in the ship
So what you do for a living ?

Jennifer Fallon

I'm an astronaut

Roland Gibert

Really

Ok so where you from ?

Jennifer Fallon

I live in space. In the International Space Station. I'm up here doing a study on goats. They don't really like the weightlessness.

Roland Gibert

Where is that I don't no it ?

Jennifer Fallon

It's in space. You know... up near the moon. Seriously, you haven't heard of the International Space Station? You've been spending too much time getting it on with those goats.

I'm on a five year mission to go boldly where no goat has gone before.

Roland Gibert

Ok nice so how much do they pay you ?

Jennifer Fallon

>Quite a lot. And so they should. I studied for years to become an Orbital Goat Herder. Can't collect my pay until I get back to Earth, though. That's in 2018.

Should be worth a lot by then.

What kind of goats are you attracted to?

Roland Gibert

Cool
You single ?

Jennifer Fallon

I work with goats in space. Of course I'm single. You didn't answer my question. What kind of goats are you attracted to?

Roland Gibert

Breed

Jennifer Fallon

You like to breed? Wow, can I ask you a question?

Roland Gibert

Yea you free

Jennifer Fallon

I'm into humans, rather than goats but Is it true that when you make love to a goat at the edge of a cliff they push back harder?

Can't get anybody to test that up here.
you know... what with the weightlessness
and all...

And no cliffs...

Roland Gibert

Don't no about that

Jennifer Fallon

Well, when you said you breed with goats
and that you were attracted to them, I
figured you know. Pity. I guess I'll have to
find someone else more useful. We're
going to lose our connection soon
anyway. Our orbit is moving away from
Africa. We'll be over the Indian Ocean
soon.

Here's a parting gift from me -
http://tinyurl.com/gotchagoatboy

[link to Romancescammers.com where his profile is flagged]

Roland Gibert

am crying

7. Scammer V Hilary Clinton... In Klingon

Gerard Joseph

Hi dear, how are you, you are beautiful, and i will love to know you more

Jennifer Fallon

who are you?

Gerard Joseph

Gerard by name

Jennifer Fallon

I can see that. Who are you? Are you a fan?

Gerard Joseph

I'm Gerard from London
what's your name

Jennifer Fallon

Are you serious?

Gerard Joseph

yes
i'm single
looking for someone who will love to

spend the rest of her life with me

Jennifer Fallon

> How can you not know my name? You just contacted me!

Gerard Joseph

> yes
> today is my first time to talk with you

Jennifer Fallon

> My name Hilary Clinton

Gerard Joseph

> nice to meet you Hilary Clinton

Jennifer Fallon

> So tell me about yourself

Gerard Joseph

> my name is Gerard
> i'm 50 years old
> with a daughter
> she is 12 years old

Jennifer Fallon

> I like piña coladas and getting caught in the rain

> I'm not much into health food, I am into champagne

Gerard Joseph

> it have been 3 years, i'm single
> good
> do you like clubbing

Jennifer Fallon

> Depends - seals or letterboxes?

Gerard Joseph

> but, when was the last day you went to club

Jennifer Fallon

> Golf clubs work well on letterboxes.

Gerard Joseph

> okay
> you like going out with friends

Jennifer Fallon

> What do you do for a living?

Gerard Joseph

> i'm engineer
> working at shipping company

Jennifer Fallon

That's amazing, I work for a shipping company, too! Which company?

Gerard Joseph

Royal Caribbean International

Jennifer Fallon

OMG! So do I!!! What are the chances! Which office do you work at?

Gerard Joseph

i can travel 3 times in a year
not always in sea

Jennifer Fallon

But which office are you based out of?

Gerard Joseph

i'm at shipping department

Jennifer Fallon

Which city?

Gerard Joseph

London

Jennifer Fallon

> Really! Me Too! How come I've never seen you around?

Gerard Joseph

> are you in London now

Jennifer Fallon

> In fact, I work in HR. I just checked. You are not on the payroll.

Gerard Joseph

> how did you check please

Jennifer Fallon

> I work for Royal Caribbean International in London. I manage all their staff. We have never heard of you.

Gerard Joseph

> sorry to say
> how long you have been working there

Jennifer Fallon

> Why are you lying about working for us? What else are you lying about?

Gerard Joseph

my dear
are you sure, you are working with the company
or you are once with them

Jennifer Fallon

Of course I'm sure, you idiot! Ring them and check. Ask for Hilary Clinton. I work in the office next to Bill.

Gerard Joseph

let me see your ID card
because i believe your office will have the card you use to open your Door

Jennifer Fallon

Don't be ridiculous. As if I would show a complete stranger on the internet - who is already proved to be a liar - my ID card. Call them now. the number is 0844 493 4005. Ask for Hilary Clinton.
You can talk to my secretary. Her name is Monica.

Gerard Joseph

i want to understand a point here, are you in London as i speak, or another country

Jennifer Fallon

Call me at the office and find out.

Gerard Joseph

i will give my boss
because he knows every member in this company

Jennifer Fallon

What's your boss's name?

Gerard Joseph

Michael Campbell

Jennifer Fallon

I just spoke to him. He says he's never heard of you either.

Gerard Joseph

give me the office number
you used to call him now please

Jennifer Fallon

I though he was your boss? You should know it by heart.

Gerard Joseph

> but, you said you speak to him now
> let me know who you called
> maybe you are calling a different people
> that is not the same company with us

Jennifer Fallon

> Hahahaha

Gerard Joseph

> i don't understand why you are laughing
> just give me the number you called now

Jennifer Fallon

> You are too funny!

Gerard Joseph

> really
> tell me where you are working at
> i have checked your information in FB, is
> saying a different thing
> and what you telling me now

Jennifer Fallon

> OK... you got me. I don't really work there. Iwork for the FBI.

Gerard Joseph

i understand
this is how FBI people do
you want to scary me away
not to talk to you

Jennifer Fallon

Given your terrible grasp of English, I'm
not sure we can call this "talking"

Gerard Joseph

you can call it anything
but it's chat
you can use any language that comes to
your mind to answer

Jennifer Fallon

How's your Klingon?

Gerard Joseph

cool
and yours

Jennifer Fallon

Heghlu'meH QaQ jajvam [It's a good day
to die]

Gerard Joseph

sorry

what does this means

Jennifer Fallon

I thought you spoke Klingon?

Gerard Joseph

i speak only one language
and that is English

Jennifer Fallon

See... lying again! You said you spoke
Klingon! naDevvo' yIghoS! [Go away]
I'm going to have to report this to Star
Fleet

Gerard Joseph

my dear I'am British i was born at St
James hospital, and i never learn how to
speak other country language
what i speak is English

Jennifer Fallon

You speak bullshit
You are not even in London. I can trace
your IP address.

Gerard Joseph

> do that
> and tell me where my location are

Jennifer Fallon

> You don't know where you are? Look out the window

Gerard Joseph

> i don't know
> i will like you to tell me please

Jennifer Fallon

> Why?

Gerard Joseph

> i want you tell me, where my IP address is

Jennifer Fallon

> Why?

Gerard Joseph

> you said you will track my IP address
> i want you do that, and tell me where is my location

Jennifer Fallon

> Why?

Gerard Joseph

> you make everything appear i'm talking shit

Jennifer Fallon

> Geez... ya think?

Gerard Joseph

> i want to ask you a question

Jennifer Fallon

> Make it quick... I'm bored with you now

Gerard Joseph

> do you like making jokes

Jennifer Fallon

> Like you wouldn't believe

Gerard Joseph

> i ask
> because i'm seen it as joke,or to scary me away not to talk to you
> that's why i ask

Jennifer Fallon

> It's because you're a scammer and while

you are talking to me, you are leaving some other poor woman alone.

Gerard Joseph

Sorry

Jennifer Fallon

So you should be

8. Scammer V Transgender 87 Year-Old

Alexander Williams

>Hello

>How are you doing

>I hope we meet up and talk one day

Jennifer Fallon

>Why? Are you a fan?

Alexander Williams

>Sorry for missing you

Jennifer Fallon

>Who are you?

Alexander Williams

>A friend,I wish we meet and talk more

Jennifer Fallon

>Where do you live?

Alexander Williams

>I'm a mixed race from New Zealand and Brazil

how are you doing

Jennifer Fallon

I'm fine. Who are you?

Alexander Williams

I'm Alexander from New Zealand and Brazil but stays at the states

What of you

I think facebook suggested you for me

Jennifer Fallon

Facebook decided we were a match? That's great. I didn't realize it was so helpful. I had all sorts of trouble after I changed my gender from male to female.

Alexander Williams

What do you mean by that

Are you saying you did it male here

Jennifer Fallon

I used to be a man. Now I'm a woman.

Alexander Williams

what happen

Jennifer Fallon

I had an operation. What are your feelings toward transgender people. Are you understanding or a bigot?

Alexander Williams

Oh,Now I got that

Why do you did that,If I may ask

Jennifer Fallon

If you understood what it is to be transgender, you would not need to ask. You're not very sensitive or caring, are you?

Alexander Williams

I'm nice meeting you

I hope we know each other well here

Jennifer Fallon

We're not going to know each other at all until you can demonstrate you have some concept of my position and my status. Please provide me with a brief explanation of your understanding of what it is to be transgender and the current issues facing people like me.

Alexander Williams

HMM

Jennifer Fallon

That is not an answer. I do not think you are a genuine person. I think you are a scammer looking for vulnerable women.

Alexander Williams

No,but I don't get what you mean by that and I have never seen that before

Jennifer Fallon

How can you say that? Where do you live?

You must live in a cave somewhere!

Alexander Williams

I live in the states I have hear about that but to be honest I have not even get a little time to know about that

Hello,Are you here ?

Jennifer Fallon

No way... you cannot be that ignorant and live

in the Western Hemisphere. I'm not sharing anything with you. How about you answer some of my questions? How old are you?

Alexander Williams

hey,Why are you saying that I'm ignorant

I'm 53years and what of you

If just that my job does not keep me home so much

Jennifer Fallon

Because you have never heard of a transgender person. Why do you answer all my questions with other questions?

Alexander Williams

I have heard but I don't have much ideas about that

So how old are you too

Jennifer Fallon

Bullshit. You don't even know what it is. You just said you had never heard of it. Are you a liar as well as ignorant?

Alexander Williams

I told you that I have heard about that but does not know much about that

Jennifer Fallon

Look it up on YouTube

Alexander Williams

okay,I will do that

So How old are you now ?

Jennifer Fallon

I am 87

Alexander Williams

Okay,But you look so young than your picture over here

Are you the one here as your profile picture

Jennifer Fallon

Everybody lies on the internet. I'll bet you don't look anything like your picture, either.

Alexander Williams

lol

why are you saying that

That is me and I will never do that

Jennifer Fallon

Really? Because your photo is listed on a whole bunch of scammer sites with a warning attached to it.

Alexander Williams

Me....why did you find that and how come

Jennifer Fallon

Because I am not an idiot and it's really easy to check these things.

Alexander Williams

I know that but where did you find that

Can You tell me where you find this so I can get there and check

Jennifer Fallon

No. Go find it yourself...

It's not hard. You're all over the Internet.

Ever considered another line of work?

Alexander Williams

You are lieing and I don't believe you

Where did you get that information form and I want to know and go check it now

Jennifer Fallon

That's your problem, sweetie, not mine. The only reason I'm still talking to you is because I rang the police to say I'd found you and they're tracing this conversation so they told me to keep you talking. What's the weather like there?

Alexander Williams

okay,I will like that and when they find me I will speak with my lawyer

Why do think I'm a coward

I don't believe you

I will never do such a thing and I charish what have

Jennifer Fallon

Charish is not a word

Alexander Williams

Is not what you have that can take care of me or my kid

But what

What ever way you get that

Do you know how long I have used this account and you here telling me this kind of shit

Do you know how many friends that I have over here who are police who have never tell me ths

What do you take me for

Jennifer Fallon

You started the account 1 month ago.

And where exactly is "here"

Actually it was two weeks ago. Not bad too get listed in that short a time.

Maybe you should have used a photo that other scammers aren't using too

Alexander Williams

What do you mean by that

hey you can't get in here and been telling me shit

Jennifer Fallon

You contacted me, dipshit

Alexander Williams

What a hell are you talking oif

You are rather a scammer

You go away

9. Very Focused Scammer V The Dominatrix... And The Cia

Tom Gibson

> Hello Angel how are you doing here today?...I feel blessed meeting someone so beautiful and smiling as you here to day. I wouldn't trade that smile for anything. I don't know you, I was searching for an old friend, when i stumbled on you, I got entangled in that wonderful smile, couldn't stop myself from saying hello. Please always wear that smile.

Jennifer Fallon

> Did you know that an introduction like that makes you sound like some kind of sex predator on the prowl for vulnerable women. Just saying.

Tom Gibson

> dear i look at your lovely pictures you are pretty and i will love to know you better
> What a nice and sparkling smile. I wouldn't trade that smile for anything. I don't know you, I was searching for an old friend, when i stumbled on your profile. I got entangled in that wonderful smile, couldn't stop myself from saying hello. Please always wear that smile.

Jennifer Fallon

That's amazing. I've had three other random guys tell me the same thing this morning. Are you an oil company engineer, too?

Tom Gibson

no but i must say this you are beautiful and will love to know you more better

Jennifer Fallon

What do you do?

Tom Gibson

can you tell me more about your self

Jennifer Fallon

No. I want to know about you.

Tom Gibson

I am a construction Engineer

Jennifer Fallon

Who do you work for?

Tom Gibson

are you asking all thing question

Jennifer Fallon

Because you are asking me questions. Why can't I know about you?

Do you have something to hide?

Tom Gibson

I am a construction Engineer,I specializes in Roads and Building construction company and industrial building in and outside of England were do you live and what do you do for a living?

Jennifer Fallon

I am self employed. I am a Dominatrix.

Tom Gibson

are you married do you have kids?

Jennifer Fallon

Are you married?

Tom Gibson

no i am not married i am a widower

Jennifer Fallon

Me too. My husband died from eating an arsenic

laced sandwich about a year ago. Fortunately, they were never able to prove who gave it to him. Have you been a naughty boy?

Tom Gibson

how long have you been a widowed do you have kids?

Jennifer Fallon

Are you thick? I just told you that. Geez... how did you ever get though university?

Tom Gibson

okay so sorry i get you now a year ago do you have kids?

Jennifer Fallon

Why does that matter? Don't you like kids?

Tom Gibson

i love kids i have a loving and caring daughter Jessy

Tom Gibson

do you have pet do you live alone what are your fun and favorite things?

Jennifer Fallon

Good for you. I hate the little buggers. Never had

kids, don't want them.

Tom Gibson

> wow my daughter is lovely and pretty we will love to meet her
> tell me more about your self

Jennifer Fallon

> I am a Dominatrix

Tom Gibson

> What are some of your goals hopes and dreams? How long have you been single ? Do you have any brothers or sisters?

Jennifer Fallon

> I think we need to talk about my job before we get into something so personal. How do you feel about what I do for a living? It tends to put some guys off. Others just want to be spanked.

Tom Gibson

> i am okay with your job tell me more about it

Jennifer Fallon

> Very rich men pay me to dress up in thigh high leather boots and whip them with a riding crop because they've been naughty. Have you been

naughty?

Tom Gibson

no dear

i am okay with you i want a woman in my life who will love me with her heart and will do anything to make her man happy
your job is not important i want your heart and true love care

Jennifer Fallon

You're kinda missing the point about being a dominatrix, dude. YOU have to make ME happy, not the other way around.

Tom Gibson

i understand all you have said now not mad about you i understand but i will love to ask you a question?

Jennifer Fallon

OK

Tom Gibson

i will love to know if you have some one in your life and if you are in love with some else?

Jennifer Fallon

No. I do not have a boyfriend. Or a partner.

Tom Gibson

I guess am blessed to come across you am interested in you, I don't go around with bad feelings....I am an open book
do you like my photo? i love your picture you are so beautiful

Jennifer Fallon

I love your photo. I also love that it appears on at least 3 different web profiles as a scam. You must be very popular if all those sleazy scammers are using your photo to rip off women. They are using your name, too. I guess that's what you get for being an open book.

Tom Gibson

what that why i do not have more pictures here thanks

tell me about your family and what you like and dislike?

Jennifer Fallon

Hang on... aren't you worried about these scammers abusing your good name?

Tom Gibson

i understand but i have to stop posting my photo thanks how did you get to know about that how did you check

Jennifer Fallon

One of my clients is very high up in the CIA. He checks on everything for me. He's worried I'll get scammed, so he checks out everyone I talk to on line. If they are not legit, he "takes care of them" for me, if you know what I mean. After he tells me what he's arranged to have done to them, I get to spank him for being a naught boy. It's an ideal win-win situation, don't you think?

Jennifer Fallon

He's probably tracing this line now. It's so comforting having good friends like that.

Tom Gibson

wow that nice

Jennifer Fallon

Isn't it just? Good thing you have nothing to worry about. They still haven't located the last guy who tried to scam me:)

Tom Gibson

that good tell me more about your self and your family? are you on any dating site

Jennifer Fallon

Hang on... my CIA friend is ringing me on my cell. Back in a minute...

Tom Gibson

how i will love to know about it? the scam

Jennifer Fallon

Hello?

Where did you go?

Tom Gibson

i am here so how did it go

[Invited my "CIA friend" to join the chat]

Jennifer Fallon

Hi David

https://www.facebook.com/tom.gibson.1253236

David

> This is Agent Smith from the CIA (Internet Security Division) - State your name and Address immediately!

> **[Tom disappears off-line]**

Jennifer Fallon

> Tom? Hello?

10. Scammer v The Interpol Investigator

Steve Johnson

Hi how are you doing,Am Steve Johnson i really like your beauty when i saw your pictures here, can we be friends..write me back if you find me interesting,What is your Email so that will can communicate to know each other, Have a nice day

Jennifer Fallon

How do I know if you are interesting or not? I don't know anything about you. Are you rich?

Steve Johnson

am steve and am a business man

Jennifer Fallon

What sort of business?

Steve Johnson

engineer

and you?

Jennifer Fallon

That's a profession, not a business. What type of engineer are you? I know lots of different types of engineers, what is your field of expertise?

Jennifer Fallon [10 hours later]

What happened? One minute you're in love with my photo and as soon as I starting asking a hard question like WHAT SORT OF ENGINEER ARE YOU? you disappear!

Steve Johnson

am a civil Engineer

what about you ?

Jennifer Fallon

I am a special criminal investigator for Interpol. I track down scammers targeting vulnerable women on the internet. Very cool job. We have the technology now to pinpoint a scammer's exact GPS location, just from their Facebook chats.

Steve Johnson

wow

that is very good

Jennifer Fallon

It is... scammers are so sneaky. They set up profiles with no other friends... like... OMG like yours! Sorry. I have to report this to my superiors. You might be a scammer. I'm sure you're not, but if you could just wait at that address for the next three hours, the police will be there and you can show them your ID. Once they know you're legit, you'll be fine. Sorry about this but it's my job and you have to be so careful these days. Will you wait for the police?

Jennifer Fallon

Steve? Are you still there?

Steve?

11. Scammer v The Jail Bird

Loving Heart

> Wow you have bright and fascinating smiles.who did you inherit this beautiful smiles from your dad or your mom lol

Jennifer Fallon

> hello

Loving Heart

> how was your day?
>
> i really would like us to get to know more about each other but am not always here on FB so i was thinking if it would be matured for us to texting each other on mobile what do you think?

Jennifer Fallon

> Sorry, we're not allowed to have mobile phones here in prison

Loving Heart

> do you return home from we can text when you get home or do you spend your entire day at the prison?

Jennifer Fallon

> I won't be out for another 5 years. Maybe I'll get

parole then.

Loving Heart

wow what got you into prison?

Jennifer Fallon

I met this guy on the internet and he scammed me out of a lot of money so I hunted him down and shot him. Apparently that's illegal. He won't scam anyone else, though. That's for sure.

Loving Heart

wow that is very sad were was he from?

Hello are you there?

Jennifer Fallon

Sorry... they monitor our Internet conversations here. Warden says you look suspicious. Can you please provide your current address, driver's license number and social security number? Once they've checked you out, we'll be allowed to keep on chatting. I'd like to. You say you like my smile. It's going to look even better when I get out of here and have the teeth replaced that Big Bertha knocked out in a fight last month.

Jennifer Fallon

Hello?

12. Scammer v The Grammar Nazi

Mogan Marta

Hello and how are you doing today..

Jennifer Fallon

Who are you?

Mogan Marta

I am mogan..and you

Jennifer Fallon

You contacted me. Why do I have to explain who I am? Do we know each other from somewhere?

Mogan Marta

Oh ok think we know one another i saw your profile oh my desktop and i like it and add you as my friend..???

Jennifer Fallon

I am a famous person. I add everyone as a friend. Don't you know who I am?

Mogan Marta

Oh yes i no and i just no that u will have a good

sense of humor...

Where are you from..

Jennifer Fallon

Seriously... I am offended that you have not heard of me. Do you not read books?

By the way, "no" in this context is spelled "know".

Mogan Marta

Oh i see and what make you mat at me..

mad at me..

Jennifer Fallon

I am not mad... I just don't understand what you want.

Mogan Marta

Oh ok and i dont want anything from you just want to no more about you and i will see were it will lead us too..

Jennifer Fallon

There is no "us". And you are not paying attention. The correct spelling of "no" in this context is "know".

What on earth makes you think you and I have

some sort of future when you don't even use the words "no" and "know" correctly?

Mogan Marta

Oh dont be scared and where are from..

Where are you from..

Jennifer Fallon

I am not scared. I am just looking for an independently wealthy man with a basic grasp of grammar. Why do you keep asking where I am from? It's right in front of you on my Facebook page.

Mogan Marta

OH I SEE

PLZ CANT YOU TELL ME NOW WHERE ARE YOU FROM

Jennifer Fallon

Why??? It's right in front of you?

And it's spelt "please" not "PLZ".

Also, it's rude to type in all capitals. It's the Internet equivalent of shouting. Why are you shouting at me?

Jennifer Fallon

Hello? Still there?

13. Scammer v The Gold-Digger

Harry Leo

hello dear

Jennifer Fallon

Who are you?

Harry Leo

i am Harry Leo by name

Jennifer Fallon

I can see that. Why are you contacting me?

Harry Leo

thank for accepting my friend request. i don't known you in person, i was searching for an old friend when i stumbled on your profile. i got entangled on that wonderful smile, couldn't stop myself for saying hello!! i will like us to get to know each other more better dear

Jennifer Fallon

Let's start by you not calling me "dear". It's creepy.

Harry Leo

sorry about that

Jennifer Fallon

What makes you assume I want to know you better?

Harry Leo

you are very beautiful and you have a captivating smile

it will be my pleasure to get to know you better

Jennifer Fallon

I'm sure it would be. As you say, I am very beautiful. What's in it for me? You are not nearly as beautiful as I am and I don't find your smile the least bit captivating. Are you rich? I could get past my dislike for your physical appearance if you have lots of money.

Jennifer Fallon

Hello... Harry... are you still there?

Harry Leo

hello

am sorry i was busy, am preparing dinner

Jennifer Fallon

You didn't answer my question. Are you rich?

Harry Leo

are you after riches?

Jennifer Fallon

I have already been married four times. The last one didn't leave me enough life insurance. I am looking for a man with lots of life insurance. Do you have a large insurance policy and are you allergic to peanuts, by any chance?

Harry Leo

am not allergic to peanuts

Jennifer Fallon

Oh... that's a pity. Do you have any allergies? Also, do you have children. It's always difficult when there are children.

Jennifer Fallon

Little buggers think the insurance money ought to go to them...

Harry Leo

i am 51 years of age a widower, and also a Swedish but i relocated to London here in United Kingdom (UK) when i was still very younger with my Forster parent, i am a ship engineer

Jennifer Fallon

Cool... so is your job dangerous?

Harry Leo

I lost my wife 4years ago since then i have been so concern with my job, also i have a lovely son called jerry who will be 9 in a couple of months

i do rather use the word adventurous

Jennifer Fallon

With a 9 year old, you're not a very good prospect. Who looks after your kid while you're at sea?

Harry Leo

he is in Borden school

Jennifer Fallon

Borden School. Do you mean Lizzie Borden School? She is my hero.

Harry Leo

no

Thomas's Preparatory School

Jennifer Fallon

Nice school. Will they let him stay over the holidays

if I want to holiday on the ski fields in Switzerland without him?

Harry Leo

ok dear

Jennifer Fallon

That's useful. I like men prepared to abandon their children so they can holiday with complete strangers. Do you have any other morals that might get in the way of us having a relationship?

Harry Leo

i can't abandon my son

Jennifer Fallon

But you just said you would.

Harry Leo

i love him so much, and anyone that want to have a relationship with me, will also accept my son too

that wasn't what i meant

Jennifer Fallon

That's good to know. You are such a good dad. I will ring the school and tell them. Jerry Leo is your son's name, right? Hang on a minute. I have the number here...

Harry Leo

why would you want me to abandon my son?

Jennifer Fallon

Why are you still talking to me? And you haven't yet convinced me you are rich enough for my attention.

Jennifer Fallon

And why do you have no friends on Facebook and only belong to Indonesian Business Associations? Are you a scammer, too? Dude, you need to build a better profile. You're never going to get anywhere with a FB page like that! They'll spot you for a fake a mile away! You haven't even liked your fake kid's school page.

Jennifer Fallon

I could give you some pointers... it's how I met my last 4 husbands...

Jennifer Fallon

Harry?

14. Scammer v I Don't Have Time For This Anymore

Michael Myers

How are you doing? I am new here and searching profiles,I try to sense a match in us and would love to see if something good comes up from this. I am Michael and single. I really like your profile and found both of us compatible to a reasonable extent.Well am looking for a caring and loving woman who can take good care of me, that I can also take good care of her as well. It's hard to put down in words what you think you may be looking for in someone, because sometimes you don't know what you are looking for until you stumble across it.i really will appreciate getting to know you more if you share the same motive on here as i do. hoping to read from you soonest.

Mike

Jennifer Fallon

Fuck off

15. How do I spot a Scammer on Facebook?

1. Terrible Spelling and Grammar

For a lot of Scammers, English is a second language. And it shows. They have terrible grammar and their punctuation is often non-existent.

2. Brilliant, poetic writing

Does it sound like this man is as sensitive and understanding as a poet? Google his heart-warming words and find out who he stole them from.

3. He likes your smile (eyes, nose, freckles, etc...)

My profile photo

Hi how are you doing, Am Steve Johnson i really like your beauty when i saw your pictures here, can we be friends..write me back if you find me interesting,What is your Email so that will can communicate to know each other, Have a nice day

4. Let's go somewhere we can be alone

Scammers need to get you off the legit sites as soon as possible. They don't want anybody else seeing what they're up to. Asking for your email, cell number or any other form of communication is a huge red flag.

Never, ever give him your physical address!

If you are online dating, the smart thing to do is to create a unique email address with Gmail or yahoo, so if you need to cut off communication, you can just delete the address.

5. His profile was set up recently and he has no friends (or only female friends)

Scammers steal other users photos/identities and they're smart enough to pick "ordinary" men. They don't look like Brad Pitt. They look like the guy next door. Try using <u>Google Goggles</u> to search to see if the photo can be found elsewhere online Watermarks mean they lifted the shot from an online photo library.

If they only have female friends, rest assured, they are the other women he's scamming, just like you!

Want proof? Ask for a live video talk using Skype or Facetime, and don't accept that he doesn't have a camera. You can't buy a smartphone, tablet or laptop without one.

6. He has a job that takes him to exotic places. A lot.

Scammers often claim to have professional jobs (engineer, UN negotiator, etc.) that require them to be out of touch for extended periods. It's also a reason for them to later ask you to wire them funds to Western Union, as soon as they think they have reeled you in.

7. I like your photo… we must be soul mates

Scammers will claim a "connection" with you, either spiritual or physical, based on the quality of your profile photo. Always fun when you've actually posed a picture of your cat.

Don't fall for what seems to be everything you have ever wanted in a man – he can read your profile and get what you want to hear, just from what you've posted online.

8. Where are you from?

Very early on, he will ask where are you from, even if your page has a StreetView map of your location. Don't tell them. Even if he is legit, if he's too stupid to read what's on the screen in front of him, it's not worth having even an Internet fling with!

9. He wants money

I'm desperate. The bank is closed. I've been robbed. A corrupt official stole my money…. Don't believe any of them. If he's as well-heeled as he'd like you to believe, he's got other friends he can hit up for cash in an emergency.

ABOUT THE AUTHOR

Jennifer Fallon is the author of 17 full-length bestselling novels and a number of published short stories in genres ranging from horror to science fiction.

In addition to 4 complete fantasy series - The Demon Child trilogy, The Hythrun Chronicles, the Second Sons Trilogy,The Tide Lords Quadrilogy and the Rift Runners series - Fallon has written both a tie-novel and short fiction for the TV series, Stargate SG1, an official Zorro story, a novella for the Legends of Australian Fantasy Anthology and has a superhero - The Violet Valet (CHICKS IN CAPES).

Fallon has a Masters Degree from the Creative Arts faculty of QUT. A computer trainer and application specialist, Fallon currently works in the IT industry and spends at least a month each year working at Scott Base in Antarctica.

Other titles by Jennifer Fallon

Writing as Jennifer Fallon:

Second Sons Trilogy
The Lion of Senet
Eye of the Labyrinth
Lord of the Shadows

The Hythrun Chronicles

Wolfblade Trilogy — *Demon Child Trilogy*

Wolfblade Trilogy	Demon Child Trilogy
Wolfblade	Medalon
Warrior	Treason Keep
Warlord	Harshini

The Tide Lords
The Immortal Prince
The Gods of Amyrantha
The Palace of Impossible Dreams
The Chaos Crystal

Writing as JJ Fallon
MacReadie v The Love Machine

Jennifer's Latest Series:

The Rift Runners Trilogy

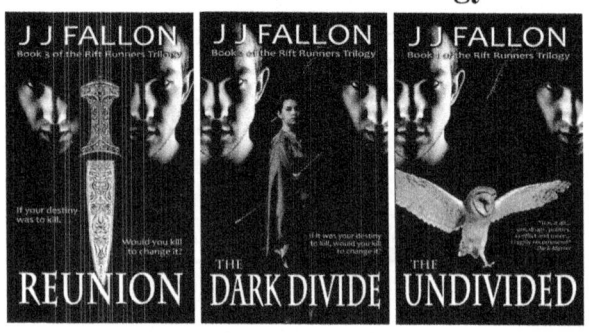